Graffiti Blowback

Poems In Mutant English

James Goodson

iUniverse, Inc.
Bloomington

Graffiti Blowback
Poems In Mutant English

iUniverse books may be ordered through booksellers or by contacting:

iUniverse
1663 Liberty Drive
Bloomington, IN 47403
www.iuniverse.com
1-800-Authors (1-800-288-4677)

Because of the dynamic nature of the Internet, any web addresses or links contained in this book may have changed since publication and may no longer be valid.

Any people depicted in stock imagery provided by Thinkstock are models, and such images are being used for illustrative purposes only.

Certain stock imagery © Thinkstock.

ISBN: 978-1-4502-9316-7 (sc)
ISBN: 978-1-4502-9315-0 (ebk)

Printed in the United States of America

iUniverse rev. date: 1/19/2011

1 CYBER SODOMY CRASHING

Or Watching The Great Divide Of The Real
From The Synthetic I.T. Boys. The Syn-Droids
Would Perform The Annual Initiation Ritual Of Anal Probing
In Their Herd-Mind Think-Link Binary Fraternity
While They Collectively And Quantitatively Interfered
With My Serious Ambitions Of Becoming A Dirty Old Man.

THOSE WHO THINK THEY ARE REAL:

In Module #1

Eli.com pounds out a program
As his smile sinuously wraps around his unbounded ripeness.
But he sneers in fearful disdain at his gay face
While he carefully wraps his boy toys in a blanket of secrecy
And quietly hides them in the closet back in Babel, Ontario.
His frolicking hormones, however,
Tickle his nipples and laugh at his embarrassment.

But, he thinks, no one will catch him here
With his secret desire
Writhing in the prison of repression.

Please, let me not find passions boy among my friends,
He prays.

Let me stay with my wife and hide there in plain sight.

Cubicle #2

Pencil slim persnickety snit
Encapsulated in the language of his
Programming habitat,
Isolated by firewalls of
Middle class boredom while

Sunk in his rolling chair
That goes nowhere.
He has everything so right
That it died in his laptop years ago.

Perhaps it should be given
A proper funeral in the Cyberville Mausoleum
Of obsolete ideas that never really worked.
Then you might pray,
"He leadeth me thru the Gateway Tower
Where surely my dongle shall dangle
In the valley of the Dell,
And dwell in the infinite loop."
"This is solely FYI ."

He's Down the Hall
Second Door on the Right

Hulking over the underbelly
Of suspicious doings in the video library
Hugging the old stand-byes that
His daddy beat him with
When he tried to talk back.
"My daddy said . . .
And then he told me …
And I learned everything I had to know from him.
And I'll smash anybody's otherwise
Who says different. . .
Because that's how to be a man.
Screw the marines
They're right as rain
Bugger the sergeants
If they didn't say so too.

Now, with a middle aged spread and
Armed with a wireless quicksilver keyboard in his hands
And a well worn skateboard in his brain

He wanders about in the smoking zone outside
On his fifteen minute morning break wondering,
"Why am I still alone?"

Johnny Heckle Freckle

He wraps his slithery, flickering tongue
Gently around the minds of his friends
And coats their listless thoughts
With agreeably venomous slime.

He, very privately, skinnys up his own flag pole
And never tells about his shadowy fantasies.
They would betray him
Throw a spotlight on his comfortable darkness.

He is so careful, by day, about his whiz-kid,
Normal Christian façade,
As American as apple pie and skin heads.
He was not educated, he was easily programmed
He did not learn, he downloaded
And is the very ditto copy of his Aryan dad,
Always ready to grab mind control
Of his buddies.

He never looks at his real face
Because he believes his own lies.
And leaves the light on at night,
So he can sleep.

For he tries to serve two masters at the same time,
But the toxic beetle juice is already flowing
Through his veins and into his dreams.

Yago

His lizard slicing incisors

Tasted exquisite as he sucked
The slime from his double split tongue.

His neurons raced through the
Transistors he had for brains.

He thrived on delicious envy
As it wrapped around
His plans like a ribbon in the wind.
Like rust around a magnet

His self inflation would multiply
In gigabytes when he gently
Closed his eyes to see
"Great gay genius dude"
Blinking in neon lights across his vision.

There is nothing that can
Destroy or penetrate his fortress
Of self adulation.
It upgrades itself
Automatically each calendar year.

THOSE WHO ARE REAL:

Align Alika Allen

A nice kid, a jock and a nerd
A nice kid, though he's part of the herd.

Brawny little butthead
Walks a straight course
All of the way through to the end of the line.
With his quicksilver fingers,
And flashpoint brain,
He never misses its aim.

Hey Jude Dude,

You're the loose cannon
In the elite squadron
Of keyboard cruisers.
How did your swift fingers
And gentle program
Fare in the "I Am" world of
Computer geeks caught in
The glaring gaze of Narcissus?

You disappear in honesty
Before their acquisitive reach,
But they yield to the honey comb
Of you innate realness anyway.
Potent magic in your unrehearsed charm.
Your amulet sways to forgotten music.

Wally Wunderkind

Like many aging teenagers,
Wally's first language was Binary,
His second was English.

He stares at you like a deer caught in the glare of headlights at night
But his gaze becomes the headlights as he peers inside your hollows
And lights them all up.

The amazing, short, little boy/man brainiac
With a baby face, deep voice and big feet,
Charms the machines he touches
And even people fall under his spell,
Which is cast without his knowing.

He failed the elitist test given by condescending techs
And he never knew it.
It was just not on his scanner.

The technology prodigies sorta resented him for that,
And they didn't quite know why.

It was a clean and beautiful stalemate.

Del

He is big, inside and out.
As he sits near the apex of Data Mountain
His mind orbits around the Planetary System of Alpha Tech
With a reconnaissance camera in operation 24-7
It's fun and fantastic
The world in the wires
And the wired head he keeps charged
And flying.

Paulo

As flexible as the royal palms in Rio
He leans into the complex programs
With careless ease.
He zaps the currents into life
And the whole tower hums.

The circuits offer no resistance
Unless he wants them to.
Friction does not exist in his world.
Magnetism quietly flows from his fingers
As he energizes his schematics.

His lingering gaze seems to x-ray the problems
That loom before him
As though he is being shown the way
By an ascended master from another world.

Each solution drifts through him like a beautiful spirit.

Is he really there? I don't know. I think so. I hope so.

II THE GOOD CHRISTIAN HOWDY DUDES

On A Clear Day You Can See The Muck Real Good

The homophobic down-home boys
Regurgitate their dirty minds
Onto the public walls at city hall
And inform their daddies
That they are as straight as a baseball bat
And quote,
"I am everything my daddy wanted me to be."

And then they convulsively
Spill their homemade dogma
Of four letter words on the pictures
Of their prophets.
And believe that, even though they don't go to church,
Hardly ever, almost never,
They are saved and washed
On the blood of Jesus, Pat Robertson,
Oral Roberts and Fox Cable News.
Verily, Jerry Falwell deflowered the Teletubbies
On his Sunday sermons.
That's as good as it gets.

The boys do the five finger exercise
In private, anyway, to relieve their downspouts
And slip their dipsticks in lipstick
To show they are as normal
As apple pie and skinheads.

Yeah, surely, even though Jesus
Did not say anything about
Who to have sex with,
He meant you are not supposed

To do it with another dude, dude!

Yeah, verily even though Jesus didn't say it.
You have to say it for him.
Put the right words in his mouth
And not the danged tool of some other guy.
That's the right thang to do.

The Mystic Tale of the Godda-Dos
In Honor of Mel Gibson et.al.

Once upon a time
The Catholics stole Jesus
And ran away with him.
Boo Hoo.

They stuffed him in a plaster statue
And would not let him out
No matter what. It was awful.
Boo Hoo. Boo Hoo.

They said Jesus is ours, not yours,
And you can't have him back.
Amen and halleluiah.

They said that he said:
You godda have babies
    You can't use condoms.
You godda have hetero-sex
    You can't have homo-sex.
You godda kneel down on your knees when you pray
    You can't stand up, you arrogant nobody.
You godda suffer and beat yourself up everyday
    You can't be happy because your born in sin, sinner.
You godda be one of us to get to heaven,
    You can't be a yucky protestant and do it, stupid.
And you godda vote republican.

Boo Hoo Hoo Hoo.

Oh, You Little Devil

Hiding behind your plastic Jesus face.
With itsy bitsy bits of black magic,
Everyday witchcraft for the mundane practitioners,
Tinkers, tailors, truck drivers, lawyers,
Preachers, teachers, gossipy grudgers, politicos, etc.

You utter the clichéd spells:
Son of a bitch, Mother fucker, Bastard, Asshole,
Damn you,
Go To Hell,
And so on.

You pseudo Christian inquisitors
Who use judgmental curses as a daily
Invisible sling shot on silent victims.
You expel this rotting breath with
Your foul pronouncements
And void your religious hypocrisy
With your diuretic orgasms.

You destroy self-esteem in targets with your verbal bombs.
And then go back to church on Sunday.

Denyla

The ding dong Dixie belle
Rises from her musty civil war grave
And becomes the perfect 1950s housewife. . .
Flawless, precise and in total control.
Ain't no queers, coloreds or Jews on her street.

She slimed the 60s,
Poured Clorox on the 70s,
And crossed the next few decades off her "to do" list.
So, they just didn't hardly exist in the first place.

For years, this nice little Catholic Christian lady
Weekly cleaned off the alter in her church
Where the dust collected in the cobwebs
Of her brain in its attic.

All her dreams of adventure were left
With Stewart Granger in King Solomon's Mines.
Her fantasies were strangled and buried
Under the dog house in the back yard.

Now she slowly folds into the gray of herself
With nowhere to go on her dead end street.

III THE PATCHWORK AGENDA

Fable of the Lapidary Dairy

Jasper froze in wonderment,
As he became spellbound
By the magnetic deepening of blues
In the lapis lazuli stone.
Spores of time were densely packed into a lovely solid
As they should be.
Minute particles of dinosaurs, dragons and daisies
Glistened against the light.
Reminding the dream that sleep will awaken.

The mute stone spoke of a long journey.

Jasper carefully wrapped it with thin silver wire,
Slid it onto a silken cord,
And fastened it around his neck.
Where it hung for forty years and some others,
Till it fell off into the land of lost things.

But the memory still hung from his neck
With constant sureness,
Until he fell, at last, into the same memory.

La Resume

The old girl got lost in her little black dress
After it started to breath for her.
But, no matter, it was better that way, she rationalized.

Although, she was a bit worried when she woke up
At 3 am with bits of Vogue magazine in her mouth.
No matter.

She found sleeping in the closet
Suspended from a coat hanger was
The easiest way to keep her wrinkles fresh.

With dark tinting on her car windows and
Dark sunglasses, she could drive to work
Without seeing anyone dressed in rayon
Or other debilitating synthetics.

At work in the mall,
She would don her crepe de chine battle fatigues,
Say a brief prayer at the alter of Chanel,
Take her station by the front door of the shop
And spit headlines from Women's Wear Daily
In the faces of unwary, shabby shoppers.

It was the least she could do.

Alas, she fell into a coma
When a gypsy palm reader
Told her that her lifeline ended in a thrift shop.

Chumley Dolittle III

While being sought by the detectives
Of the Tasteful Living Interpol.
He eluded and escaped over and over again,
Thus being able to continue his pursuit of calamitous creativity.

He became a wanted man in 1953
When he forcefully painted
The whole town of Houston, Texas beige.

The Decorators of America resolved
To stop his careless dictatorial designing,
Strip him of his credibility and expose him
For the tasteless fraud that he, indeed, was.

It took fifteen years, but they finally tracked him down
In his studio in the border town of Tijuana,
Where he was painting used prosthetic limbs white,
Making lamps out of them and selling them
On the Unclaimed Freight website.

Minutes of the Last Meeting

Her thoughts flowed as deep and darkly as the River Styx
While the last frayed remnants
Of blanketing darkness wrapped around her
Cozily promising extinction's final kiss,
The loss of knowing,
The end of being.

"Hooray, hooray, the wicked ole' witch is dead," they'll say.
At last, I can give them something they really want.
And if there is a God, then for God's sake
Keep that babbling nurse out of here today.
Her mindless prattle shakes broken word crumbs
All over the clean sheets on my funeral bed."

Again, she'll ask, "How are you today?"
And again I'll say, "This is still a hospice, dear,
And I'm still dying.

The only one here with a particle of sanity is that girl volunteer.
Nice, she's really nice.
And I even hate nice.
On her, it works, though.
She even shed some tears when she asked
Me if there was anything at all that I did like?
Is that a real heart beating in her pale breast?
Is there really something called love?
If so, then I'm the joke. I missed it all these years.
Old girl, I'd laugh if it didn't hurt so much."

"Yes, my tender volunteer. . .
There is something that I like. . .
There is the dawn and the bird songs.
But that's all. Not a whit more. Little enough, I say.
I await the creeping, remorseless attack of the morning light,
And the unyielding innocence of the birds' singing.

This brief encounter redeems and destroys me on its arrival.
If that is liking, then that is what I like."

"So, there you are,
And here I go.
I am done with these things,
And undone by them.
Now, leave me alone.
It is time for me to go and bury myself in the sunrise."

Her Sidelong Glance At Her Last Long Dance

The lingering wings of sorrow,
As weighted love increases,
Sigh softly upon tomorrow,
While breath slowly ceases.

Tripping lightly through the mazes,
As if there was a choice,
Wildly, desperation gazes
As fear becomes its voice.

She shreds her funeral flowers
And frantic hope betrays
Kemo dripping toxic hours
Flood her blue veined pathways.

Soul is a savage beast of light
That tears death from its lair,
It rends the veil of day and night
And lays eternity bare.

Jack

The kaleidoscopic memories exploded
As the aging soldier's heart
Opened into a blast of orchids.

He could not quite see them,
Only feel their fragile petals trembling
In his lost questions
And he began to know them again
As he found them penned
In the pages of other ancient lifetimes.

AndRue

He slowly sank into the rotting muck
Of his once brilliant intellect
Always thinking of himself as a typical New Yorker,
And fearfully denying the dark rooted fear of himself
And the bottomless pit of emptiness that lies in his void.

Now, he's blindly unaware
That he's no longer there.

Malice In Wonderland

The little green girl studies hard because
It is the only way that she can kill
The rattlesnakes in her mind.

She has to twist the truth into a hangmen's knot
So she can dissolve her slithering jealousy.
She stuffs her dead reptiles with the pages
From her straight A report cards.
And puts them beside her Barbies.

Then she dons on her nurses costume
And takes care of her suffering guilt.

Afterwards

His Last Echoes
Bonded Echoes
Binding Echoes
Echoed back to me.

I did not know him well,
But I liked him a lot.

He was short, light, tightly wired,
Taught and spring loaded.

A bunch of us knew him because
He was the handy-man, handy hands,
Know how, how to, how to do.
And he did.
He cut it, laid it, put it up
Took it down, took it apart, reamed it,
Put it back, wired it, painted it,
And fixed it good.

If it was broke, we called him.
Didn't know him well,
As well as I wanted too.
He was good, no problem.

A little guy with his head in Alpha Centauri
And his hands in junk and gunk.
I didn't know about the trap he was caught in,
That strung him out and left him dangling,
Until later. They told me then,
After they found him hanging from the attic rafters
Of the three story house he built
In North Carolina,
When it became his tomb.
Shock stopped my mind.

And broke time into little pieces
As I stood just on this side
Of the road to understanding.

I wrote a poem, lamenting his passing,
Read it to friends at his wake
And went on with my life.

But the next day at work, waves of
Twisting emotional pains
Silently drifted through me.
He knew me,
And he walked into me
Showing me the abysmal quagmire
Of his depression.
The vultures of despair began
Feeding on my raw innards.
These alien emotions took total possession of me,
Torturing me for several hours.
It all left me as suddenly as it came,
Never to cross my threshold again.

Then I knew his pain,
But not the cause of it.
Some say he had a drug problem.
I don't know.
But I did know that I was a nicely happy soul
After living some of the sorrowful plight
Of my almost friend.

The Boozing Balladeer

He was on a one-way street into the blues,
A singing rasp,
Putting down his act
In any and every stale beer joint
Around the Mississippi Delta
Always ready for a new town
And the next drunken binge.

A groaning wail in the cicada hum of night,
He would come out of the sticky, dank darkness
Singing his songs that glowed
In the garish gasses of neon bar lights,
Belly up to his other sodden buddies
To drink himself poor,
And sing for a blurry buzz
Till he could finally talk to his best friends,
The bar stools.

IV THE CONTMEPLATION STATION

C.I.S. South Beach

They found the shadow
Of the old mangrove buried
Under the Hi-Rise.

July 1st. - 3 p.m.

The dragonfly sailed
Into the sweatbox of a
Summer afternoon.

The White Heron

Thin as a moment,
It stands in quiet stillness
Outside of time's reach.

The Lyrical Scales of Fusion

The sun began a sweetly setting yawn
As I sat on the deck, holding a dry discourse with solitude.
In a dulling indifference, I rose to leave,
When a mockingbird began its evening vespers.

Its music seemed only for my hearing,
So closely falling, touching my ears
With a resonant urgency,
Just for me.

"Stay awhile please,
Or my song will fail and the sun will fall away.
Hold back the darkness for a few brief moments
So time may heal the wounds of day
And I may send my melodies soaring
To the ends of twilight
And finish my warbling breaths with your kind attention."

I leaned back, chair-bound, chained by expectancy,
The grateful prisoner of its trilling.
The magnetic creature's genetic virtuosity
Filled its fragile frame - trembling the whole of it,
Totally with a kaleidoscopic composition.

The gray-feathered breast sounding
Aspirations filled with winged sailing music.
I lost myself in the dark of its tiny pulsing throat,
Wandering momentarily on the drumming air currents,
I trembled in the downy feathers,
I paused, glazed over in its glassy eyes,
And I gripped, claw-tight, the twig perch we claimed as home.
I disappeared into its wholeness
As the bird gave it all up to the song.
I was, it was, me.
We slipped into each other in a quick touch of mindlessness

When all there was, was what it was.

There was nothing left when the song ended.
I went away with a blush of divine abandon dusting my thoughts,
As the sunset, being done, disappeared,
Quietly swathed in the shimmering veils of the evening.

The Muse of Tiredness

Let it go – let it flow
With the voices of the rain
And the secret music of the wind
The trees open their arms
And bare their souls at moonrise.
They are keepers of the sanctuary
And friends of the crawling things.
That delight in their leafings.
The mindless purpose singing
The onward go of the dancing show.

Sleep slips into the mix of this day
And infuses reality with infinity.
The dreams flash when sleep awakens.

V JOURNAL DAYS

On The Turnpike

The flush of rose tint gently extinguished
The night's lamp of darkness
And the early morning with
Massive flecks of yellow Black-Eyed Susans
Thrown carelessly about on the hills,
Lifting me out of dull apathy.

A yawing stretch of giant oaks bent low
With weeping southern moss hanging mournfully.
A mother deer ran along the roadside with her baby fawn.
Sometimes you see it, but most of the time you don't.
It's like paradise that way.

The long shadows from palms and pines
Were slowly shrinking as they fell across the highway
Where it lay stretching out to an exhausting infinity point.
The sun inch-wormed its way into the morning sky
As the signs for Disney World and Sea World blured across my eyes.
And the sun baked roofs of the tired Holiday Inn slid by on the sly.
A dollar to a doughnut, this is Orlando.

The palms and pines thinned out and disappeared in the rearview
mirror.
I glided into the hill country of lush orange groves
Carefully orchestrated in long neat rows of hand picked control.
Tiredness settled in on my head
Like a cinder block.
Many hours lay flattened behind me
And five hundred miles rose up ahead.

Driving Home From Work

Wednesday, was a lightweight fantasy of a day.
It passed so smoothly,
Things got done at work, just right.

I played the Tarot cards on the computer.
They were:
For the past; the Charioteer, a sign of accomplishment.
For the present; the Lovers, the sign of freedom and love.
For the future; the Death card, the sign of sweeping change and transformation.
The computer's horoscope said it was a day of great good fortune.

I left work a little early.
On the way home the massive clouds over the ocean
Were swollen, dark gray, rain-filled titans.
The sun was setting in the west and cast a giant rainbow over the ocean.
I could only see the first side of it as it rose up and disappeared
Into the mile-high, sodden gloom.
Hundreds of white birds swarmed in circles beneath the rainbow.
I was spell bound by the panoramic swirl of the late afternoon
And thought I should try to record it.

It was a day that seemed to whisper sweet mysteries to me over my shoulder.

Voices In The Squall

The tension finally split open the suffocating summer day
Splashing the rain against the bookstore windows in the cafe.
Coffee drinkers whispered in hushed huddles of sheltered connects,
Joined in the dry warm spaces by fragrant Colombian and Brazilian
coffee aromas.

In one clutch, a woman wearing a white tee shirt emblazoned with an
American flag sat with two teenagers who scanned their treasures of
words.
Another handsome woman in blue sweats wrote in her notebook
As she sat across from her orange haired mother.
An aging businessman propped up on his white shirt sleeved elbow
Forgot his reading, and was lost in eye vacancy, staring out into the
miniature storm.
Two dark haired girls spoke in tight harmony
While the quiet rain song splashed against their reflections in the
window.

Outside, across the patio, several people
Were sprinkled along the sidewalk beneath the movie posters.
A lot of waiting in things, next to things, and under them.
More waiting as the weather forecasts the crescendos of a thunderous
canopy
With lightning strikes from under the gray sky umbrella.

Tell me more of the small prospects and great overviews of them.
How we forget the little moments of innocence and remember the
others.
Tell me more of the distant lights
That carry us along the river's changing course in time,
And leaves us at the edge of the cosmic ocean of mysteries.

Let the rain speak.

Mundane Monday

Nothing unusual,
Very usual chores
Get rid of problems,
The boring work of staying in the flow of life.

I take a day off from work to get:
An oil change and filter for the car,
And wash and wax job, too.

I wish a can of oil, a filter, and a wash and wax job
Was all it takes to put me right.
Sixty bucks later, I'd be on the road again.
But -
I need pills for blood pressure, for blood sugar, and for cholesterol,
Ointment for a rash
Multivitamins, minerals, to shore me up
And herbal detox for dumping parasites,
And a lifetime membership to the biggest salad bar in town.

My doctor said that I tested positive
For a chronic predilection to chocolate.
It will probably, eventually "take me out."
What a way to go!

It's 9 a.m. as I sit in the car dealership waiting room
Gulping down more coffee,
Writing a "to do" list and
Trying to avoid Regis on their TV,
But he still imprints his charismatic triviality
On the deepest recesses of my sagging psyche.
I really must scan the thesaurus to find another word for "Yuck!"

I hope the car wash has CNN on their TV.
Then I can get a bi-polar attack
Watching the latest bombing in the mid-East.

To Do:
Ask my doctor for some tranks on my next visit.
Soon, I plan to get an appraisal of my extended collection of plastic pill
containers
At the Antiques Roadshow. I bet I'll be the first one to do that.
Oh yeah, the car wash has CNN on their TV.
Time for the Bi-Polar Express to come thru on the trank tracks.
Bring it on, George.
What would we do without your private, profiteering war?
Probably a lot of us would go on living, eh what?
George, do yourself a favor and
Get rid your ball and Chenny
And your compulsive taste for Rummys.

OK – now I am off to the local bank
For a sit down with formidable Frank
And get the intake and output
Of my financial lifeline to add up.
This is the part that make me shudder
And feel sorry for myself.

But not to worry,
When I get home my day is saved, at last,
By a Brit-com called "My Hero."
And two Scooby-Doo movies.

Now all is right with the world.

VI FAMILY WALLPAPER

The Momma's Boy Trilogy:

Old Images Trapped in the Scrapbook

Death once again leaves the room,
As I return to the mother's womb,
And life shuttles back and forth
Over the threads of time's old loom.

The blankness beginning,
With the endless ending,
And countless tales in between,
Forever wending.

All the philosophies on the paper page,
Turn to dust in the chamber of the sage.

Near the highway to slumber,
Where those who dwell,
Know it all and know it well,
Quickly say what dreams will tell.

From the thickness where sleep is newborn,
In glimmers, shadows and flashings,
Emerges my first memory:
Too young to crawl, helpless,
I discovered myself lying on my stomach,
Peaceful as a pillow, sucking milk from a bottle.
The afternoon shadows crawled across the shepherd and shepherdess
frolicking,
Over and over and over on the lavender meadows of the coarse
wallpaper,
In our little home behind dad's shoe repair shop.
Mother glided quietly in the room.
She put her hand in the middle of my back,

And rocked me gently,
Fading me back to sleep in the warmth of her cradling love.

Nothingness again,
Undoing all that was done,
Losing that which had been won.

The gate of my crib was outlined by moonlight
That strayed through the mosquito screening as it
Stretched across the open window and stared blankly
Out onto the backyard all soaked in the humidity
Of hovering layers of dew.
I dropped the crib gate down,
Then I dropped myself down,
Onto the sticky cool patterns floating in the linoleum.
I crawled outside and sat looking around at the new world.
The damp, scrubby patches of crab grass wet my diapers.
The water pump stayed motionless
Over the well in the middle of the yard,
The mulberry tree stood sentinel in one corner,
As the outhouse shyly hid in the other corner.

Looking up, I saw the net of stars,
Holding the night tightly around the earth,
With just enough room left to breathe.
The stars bright and burning – red, yellow, blue and white,
Seemed a lot closer then than they are now.
But that was all. The world was fenced in by time and space.
I felt captured in place where nothing else could happen.
Glittering boredom hurt. I was disappointed.
As fast as I could, I crawled back to my crib,
And went to sleep for another couple of years.

Light fell on another time. Somehow, I learned to walk one day.
It was one of the earliest of days,
One of the fresh smelling, newest of days.
I ran about the neighborhood and saw my playmate, Lois,

Sitting on the branch of a glistening spring tree.
I said hello as the lime green glow of morning,
Made us perfectly right to meet like that.
A thing could be good, too.

Then, ignorant light, blessed and bright,
Crawled back into the womb of night.

There must have been a stench,
But I couldn't smell.
Unhappily, I could feel the dread,
Of unnamable fears,
Spanning the defiled brick archways,
As live bodies were shoved into ovens.
Beings held in bonds of hopelessness,
Awaiting a firey end.
I stood in the incendiary nightmare,
Screaming, "You can't do this?"
But my voice failed utterly.
Running through the acrid vision,
My body, thinner than air, weightlessly sailed,
Through doors and walls. Helpless again,
I fell back into the safety of my crib cage,
And woke up in our little home on Humble Road.
The nightmare screams vanished in the damp Texas darkness.

The I of me probes the depths of the past with cautious intent declared.
Memories live, restless hybrid creatures,
Roaming the obscured regions of tangled trails,
In the interior of times past,
Emerging suddenly, either to bless with the virtue of wisdom gathered,
Or to devour and drag the carcass of self back to its possessive lair.
This stealth driven savage stalker of other times may rend,
The present vulnerable moment with fatal wounds,
And sentence the future to oblivion . . .

Not a place to lose my way.
But a place to explore minutely when seeking
The often hidden meaning of experience.

Each night – involuntary images.
"Now, I lay me down to sleep . . ."
My playmates, one by one,
Would peep into my mind and speak;
Bobbi said she and Alice Faye had white fox capes to dance in.
Her brother, Donald, said "Hi" and
And grinned as he dangled his dried frog from a string.
Lois said we could make colored pictures with our crayons soon.
Sandra showed me her drawing while her little sister
Tried to say something, but messed it up because of her lisp.
Their voices echoed exactly timbered in the drowsing vault where we
met.
And then the emptiness poured easily into sleep.

I tried to play jungle movie with Bobbi and Donald
In their backyard but,
I got scared when I saw a giant brown monster
Eating the houses at the end of the street.
It chased us. I ran. When I looked back it was eating their house.
I got to my house, looked in the window and saw
Mom and Dad with the neighbors gambling, smoking and drinking.
They never did that before.
The whole neighborhood was sliding down the gaping mouth of the
shapeless monster.
Stun stopped, I tried to scream a warning.
I had no voice, again, helplessness happened
As I fell all the way down,
Into the dizzying emptiness,
All the way through till I forgot what it was all about.
And what it was all about, was all about.
And I forgot.

Then the good-byes, the leave-takings and the disappearances began.

Dad was mad at F.D.R.
'Cause he got us in the war
After he said he wouldn't.
Dad and my two, all grown up brothers, enlisted,
Caught in the panic maze of soldiers, sailors, WACs and WAVESs.
Sucked up in the victimized vortex of World War Two,
They were scatter-bound around the South Pacific
Driving, diving, and flying
Ducking, dodging and outrunning
The insatiable appetite of the doomsday war machine.
We could hear the death rattles from paradise all the way back in Houston.

Within days, the house and shoe shop were empty,
The ringing voice of quietness filled the stillness,
Packed in jam-tight around the rooms that stood frozen in time.
Then, it was just mama and me.
She stubbornly kept the shoe shop doors open as a remembrance of how things had been.
She pretended to be alive
Stitching torn leather sandals back together
Re-healing worn oxfords, penny loafers, make-dos and hold-on-tos.
God willing all goes on till life was itself again.
In the cool of the evening the tin cans of rubber cement
In the shop shrank, popping, clonking and clanking.
Their sounds making a pathway through sleep with their ghostly muttering.

Each evening before curfew
The juke-box in the beer joint next door
Jarred the troubled evening
With "spurs that jingled, jangled, jingled
As those caissons go rolling along, and
A peakin' through the keyhole lookin' at Jolie Blon."

Just before shop closing time
One night, a soused-up, worn-out beer belly cowboy

Stumbled into the shop.
Threatening to go behind the counter and make love to Momma.
Helplessly, I sat watching my little legs not reach the end of the chair,
As tremors slipped down her slender boyish body.
She kept her hand clenched on the hammer,
Until his soggy, sodden lust was forgotten
When his bloated bladder made him need to go take a leak.
He wandered outside towards the ditch forgetting it all
And vanished into the night.

The traffic load on the two-lanes of Humble Road grew
By the week, day, and hour to a stream of ceaselessness,
Rumbling under the mobilizing weight of military convoys,
Carrying weapons and troops to Ellington Field
And to the overburdened train station, hissing and steaming
Like an angry dragon with a hunger for enemy blood and bones.

Road dangers sprang viscously upon straining travelers,
Halting their journeys with tombstones.
Accidents became a daily crisis of gore:
A soldier on leave making a left turn, killed instantly.
A luckless, wailing woman hit by a flying canister of gas
In a truck smash-up, had a baseball size swelling on her forehead.
A mother and her baby broadsided,
Blasted out of their car, lying, screaming, blood streaming on the ground.
Humble Road was nicknamed the Burma Road as the death toll grew.
The giant war monster sprouted wings
And came flying home to roost in front of the shoe shop.

Curfews, blackouts, and air raid rehearsals were our nightly fare.
Sometimes I'm still sitting there with Momma out on the front porch
Safely covered with a blanket of night.
Momma hides her fears from me behind an unchanging mask of calm.

But the silver, spirit-braided umbilical cord between us was not yet severed.
I heard the tears fall inside her like sighs on the wind
Betraying her strong sad composure that held true to its form.
She would not show her sorrow,
But I was bathed in it,
Anointed by her unspoken despair.

I try to close the scrapbook of time,
But the smoky fine images slip from the confines
Of pages past and 1939 says "Hello",
And 1941 becomes whole again.

My recollections are more empty and more full.
While the passing years escape more quickly.
I have to look away to reclaim the moment.

However, sometimes, I'm still sitting there
On the porch in the dark with Momma,
The two of us completing each other,
As we watch the mile high shafts of search lights
Arcing across the horizon,
Silently probing the sky
Tracing the outlines of the ominous clouds
Hoping to find them empty of disaster
And mapping the dark corners of the night
To secure them in place and make the world good again.

Early Elegy and the Frost

It isn't death; it's the dying . . .
When I think of you, so lost to us,
And to your own sweet self,
A cold wind blows through my soul with numbing sureness.
Alzheimers severs.

The crystal rain falls in pools of tears.
Spring was always there,
High in the mountains
Of another world
In another time.

I remember that it was love that brought me around again.
The grace of your simple caring pierced the armor forged by many
lifetimes,
And shattered any hardness that might be left hiding there in the
shadows.

The light of your caring made me know about love,
And remember something about forever,
So that now I can walk more surefooted on the path of life
Without the fear of sliding or falling.

But the many years have locked you away in a tower of lost memories,
And aging time tries to wrap you in a frigid shroud of emptiness.
Plagues of confusion hang like slow moving storm clouds,
In the landscape of your fading thoughts.

From this single, solitary cell of life,
That you circle like an animal trapped in its lair,
Endlessly feeling the walls
For something hidden that isn't there,
Death can only be a winged angel of freedom.

How our tired eyes fail us,

And our feeble grasp weakens over the years
Letting life slip so carelessly from our hands.

Well, then let it fail,
And then let it fall,
And in the falling,
Learn to fly.

Let it sail beyond reason,
Beyond the pain and bitter tears,
Beyond this frozen night that holds you captive.

Sail on, my darling mother.
Sail on the singing wings of the sacred sound.
Sail on to your real home in glowing, golden heart of the eternal.

The Holiday Visit

On Christmas Eve night,
While I lay half awake,
Half in a dream,
And half watching TV,
Feeling so tired and kind of old,
Mom came quietly unnoticed into the room,
And dropped a blanket over me,
Just like she did,
When I was a kid.

I slept warm, well and deep,
In the deep, warm well of sleep.

Sometime later, when I awoke,
I remembered how she forgot,
For ten years, slowly slipping away,
Into the nowhere land of Alzheimer's,
Only to die last June.

But, once again,
She remembers.

DAD:

Tom

Looking across the distance at my dad. . .
Maybe it's him, or somebody like him.
I don't know.
Because he never knew how to speak to me,
Or I to him,
So then,
I will be a child again,
And lay my head down on his shoulder in a pillow of silence.

If I could see clearly into the chamber
Where my dad stays in dreams and memories
I could see through the thickness of shoe leather,
And through some good ole' fashioned, ole' timey guilt.
I'd see creakin' farm wagons overloaded with twelve brothers
And some
Handsome
Sisters.

I'd see wild, blue eyed mountain grandpa who
Fell in an avalanche all the way down from his Latter Day Saint
pulpit
Into the smallest crumbling particles of sanity
Righteously spewing children from his loins until there was nothing
left of him.
Half way down he renounced God, until he forgot how to remember
him.
Grandma bore her life in a pure solitude of quietness,
Rapt in a shroud of acceptance
As her long straight Indian hair fell gently touching the end of her
days.

How much buckshot Bible bully bullets does it take to shoot the balls
off of a good man?

Dad was too slow to find out in time.

Few words,
Sparely spoken
And broken, less the meaning.

"Everybody knows there's stuff you've gotta say to your sons
To keep God off your butt."

Flashing fires between the forever Irish dreamer's wishes,
Never got it right as a rich hero,
And never knew why his quick tan Cherokee blood wandered in maybes,
too.

"Love's crazy enough to hate too much talkin', anyway.
Slam you hammer down hard,
And prove you're a man.
It's a good way to knock the nonsense all the way out into next week."

It was hard work for this slave of the Great Depression,
Night stalkin', timber walkin'
Ghost in a creosote plant,
And then,
A hefty sweatin', hard totin' iceman,
The happy housewives favorite hot bed and breakfast.

The last was boot making, saddles, and the rodeo.
Boy Howdy.
"As sure as there's a Mormon eatin' spuds in Idaho,
Muddy words stuck deep in the slimy creek bottom
Draw the pain of poison out of a snake's bite."

"If I had a dime for all the salt in Salt Lake City,
But we're born in Sin City,
Begatin' sin's sons,
Suckin' sin's milk,

Breathing sin's air
So sayeth the great guilt giver in the Bible belt.
Slam your slammer harder than a nail in a graveyard jail.
It just ain't gonna' go away
My son,
My purdy one."

"Now Pontiac lust
And Chevrolet fever is fine. It's just fine,
But we'd have wings if were supposed to fly."

"At least, your Mom knows enough
To straighten things out.
Don't worry.'""

The first time mom looked back at dad
Was the first time he really knew something
For the first time.
Sure nuf!

"There's a silver flower in Hiwaya
That some body stole outta my footlocker
When I was a Seabee.
I walked two miles and four years to find it.
Not too smart for an old sailor, was it?"

"Well, sonny boy,
You come in going out.
And, I guess it's my time, I gotta go now,
Over yonder where the road wanders
Into that big dense thicket of wishes it would happen,
And see where it goes.

But, you know,
What it all was,
Was not what I wanted to say.

BROTHERS:

The Two Dreams Of Tommy, Jr.

There was a boy multiplied by three,
I think it was you
I think it was me.
I think it was you and me and thee.

All thought is burned away
As the moth orbits the flame.
The real knowing is borne without a name.

In the great depression,
Tommy Jr. and Tom Sawyer went barefoot
while fishing, skinny dippin', and eating
fresh farm stolen watermelons
down on the Trinity River,
The sunlight tattooed sunburned patches on their bare knees and
butts
Right through the holes in their overalls.

How do we say good-bye to the Junkman?
He got the nickname by going for his first great dream
Which was to be a pilot in the Navy Air Corp.
But he trashed two training planes just learning to fly in World War
II.
His aircraft carrier had the cracked-up South Pacific blues.
Flying black flack shot at him splattered his nerves against the sky.
He shot the hell back, scared as a jackrabbit
And high-tailed it home
After the war.
Never did look back.

Then he jumped on his second great dream after the war,
He and his wife fired back with a family
Of three daughters and a son.

"Smart as a whip", everybody said.
Tommy should be a senator or something,"
But his family was his only dream.

Some people thought him too serious.
He loved to give a good shock to God and his crew.
He tried to convince the neighbor lady, that he was, in fact,
The Second Coming!
She panicked out and said, "Don't say that, you might not go to
Heaven."
To which he replied, "Fine, I don't wanna' go there, that's where all the
Baptists are."
He served up his corn piping hot.

His scientific inclinations did not leave much room
For any unprovable, untouchable god,
No matter how resplendent the rumors were.
He wrapped the Ten Commandments into one neat package:
"If you don't hurt yourself or anyone else when you do somethin',
You're not doing any thing wrong."
And if there was a god, Tommy, Jr.
Would have openly hated him or her or it,
After his beautiful twenty-year-old son was killed in a car wreck.
Forgiveness is a spin in a spider's web.
Nothing can be forgiven, if there is no god.

He worked behind the screen at the picture show,
Writing his own script and filming it backwards
Just for fun and because he could.
Now one knew that he knew why
The planets keep their metals inviolate caves
And turn with absolute indifference
Towards the ultimate abyss.
He knew how many times the pendulum would swing
To subtract the hours to naught.
He thought.

Faith was only for those who created god in their ego
Because they could not face
Non-existence with any intellectual grace.
Sometimes, down in the valley
A well springs clear in your mind
And heals your hurts,
Sometimes,
Sometimes not.

"God has no dominance over me.
If there is a god, it is my wife or
My daughters
Or my dead son
Or my little dog, "Buddy".
But it is not, quote, God, unquote".

The hurt that runs deep
And never stops
Paints a vivid portrait of your god
That isn't there.
At first, I cried,
Now, I just laugh."
The fire that burns in Tommy Jr. lights his darkness
With the clarity of his mental courage.

"Try to be yourself,
It takes a long time to be yourself
Because first you have to find out who you are.
That may take some doin',
All your life maybe.
You are not anybody else
You are the one and only you."

I have to keep reminding my family and my friends
That I am damn near perfect,
Because they forget so quickly.
If Einstein and Hawkins can't prove it, it is not a reality,

Don't make fairytales do for the real thing."

When the creaking door opens and
The blinding light falls on the innocent,
The babe is wrapped in swaddling robes of the new dawn
And the old rattler slithers away
Into the past.
How then will the bells ring without smiling?
Then the trumpets will sound a tidal wave to carry us home
Past the time of thinking
And past the time of dreaming?
Whispered words float away unspoken.

"Folks, save your savior sermons,
Don't waste 'em on me.
Oblivion is going to be my last friend.
I can embrace infinity
But never, forever and always.
You're only as high as your mind can reach", he thinks.

Brought down by cancer,
He dies in the opiated Hospice bed
Trying to read the invisible words
On the empirical wall that surrounds his mind,
And ponder on the burning door he left behind.

I think
On some far day
When we are all blown away
I'll turn to him and say
"I told you so."
There was a boy multiplied by three
But we all know that can't be.

Charley Road Away

His animal spirit-guide whispered across the water
So that it would not be forgotten,
Or go the way of the vapors.
And Charley came back as a one-eyed truck driver.

When I was still a kid, he said,
Grandpa Goodson sat me on his knee
And told me how six of his brothers
Were hung in Mississippi for cattle rustling',
And he told me how grandma
Was the daughter of a Cherokee princess.
And how she would go out in the woods
And find sassafras roots to make tea with.
And told me how he used to be a Latter Day Saint preacher,
And how my dad and mama had to elope
Because everybody thought the Latter Day Saints
Were Mormons with a lot of wives.
He told me how he lost God and didn't want him back.

There is always a lot of midnight.

When I grew up,
I made up a new team,
Benny, Willy and me.
Benny kept me up,
And Willy kept me happy.

I super sized my will,
Worked Willie to the bone,
And drove Benny hundreds of thousands of miles
Around this good ole' country.

I was my truck when I made a long haul,
I had a road map of the United States
Printed all over my brain.

I could see it when I was asleep.
Gravel and tar can take you far.
I was my axel and my engine
And I ate the oil can for breakfast.
All I wanted was a couple of million dollars,
A ranch in East Texas,
Two six packs of Budweiser a day
Some unfiltered Camels
And as much good sex as Willy could deliver.

Singin' about my hanker,
Driving my ole' tanker
Yankin' on my whanker
Gotta go and thank 'er
Yo ho ho
And a brew to go.

Midnight was a good number,
I always raided the hen house then,
And planted potatoes if the moon was on the wane.
There's always enough midnight goin' around
To give everybody a dead man's dose.

The darkness is as hard as a brick wall.
All the days seems lost in it,
Swallowed up in it,
I can't seem to get out of it,
Or climb over it.
So, I steal what pleasure I can
And suck the big breast of time
Have sex with it
Blow my self off into nothing.
Die there for a moment and
Come back to life.
Then hit the road again
With all 18 wheels rolling
And keep on going

Using the distance as a gauge
To number my days here
In the dark hardness.

You gotta have more sense than a brick wall.
Most of the time I do.
But do what I say,
Not what I do.

I get away with it,
I get away.
No point in only having one good eye
And one glass eye
If I can't brag about it.
It's a good thang I'm so good looking.

I wander around a lot
And I wonder why wonder.
There's more questions than answers,
So why ask in the first place
When you couldn't understand most of it anyway.
A lotta mind bother to make you crazy
And being crazy is a waste of time.

Blow me away, my lad
I don't want to stay
Any old way.
Just gimme a couple of million to spend
And I'll be done with this old world.

Good by is just as good as Hello.

VII DOG TAGS

X-ray Of The Trapping Wrappings

I seem to be the possessive canister
That grips tight, in containment,
Life's body tension held
As the face grabs the skull
And the masque suctions onto the soul.

The mirror holds me as well
As me to my own person.
The somber music of the calliope
Is just out of earshot . . .
Of the merry-go-round of being.

Dodging The 66 Year Old Phantom, And Then Some

The History Colossus stands spanning time
With one foot in the past and one in the present,
Gaining the advantage, obscuring the purpose of now
And vaporously hiding that which lies ahead.

He spins his ancient power,
Amid tons of fallen rubble,
Scattered indiscriminately.
Slag piles ghostwrite my diary again and again,
Leaving enough shocked debris in its wake
To fuel Sherlock Holms' feverish need for discovery.

In the climber's backpack lies
A day or two
Stretched out like doorways
To enter and recover
Original moments.

Looking backwards baggage
Whizzing around in the circling gyroscope of memory,
Recapturing thoughts with corrosive snares
More real than the present.

Or are they?

I remind myself,
"What you see is what you get."
So I strain to pierce the gauze of dulling apathy
Webbed around the sound of clarion calls
As the silver melodies awaken the remembrances
Of looking homeward once more.

Shadow Play – Who Am I?

Act One:
Look closely, my angel.
Excuse me, but who was that masked man?

Convergence, like lightning, strikes
As I wander backwards thru the mirror
Corroded with time's oxidized burnishings.
I slowly catch up with myself,
Catching up with myself
At last, long last.

Sorry I was me times,
Sorry I am times,
Glad I was there times,
Happy to be me times,
Flow silver, silken memories
Thru the stacks of ages,
In my aging pages.

Who was he,
That am I,
And I, who was he?
I am not yet that,
Not quite yet,
But soon.

Set your watch me closely, my angel,
Watch me and see.
My timepiece is failing.

Act Two:
While peering through the mask,
A wish to fall with the rain
Cool and thrilled with falling
Silent on the wind's breath

In water's communion,
Free from memory

The blue rain fell,
The blue rain falls,

I pretend I see it,
Then I do see it,
The rain falls in my desire
And my thoughts are
Misty whispers of relief
Rising from the graves of then
And resting on the pure air of now.
The early morning remembers
To let the first rays of light
Stir amnesia among the ruins
And raise the ashes to life again
Among the immortals.

The game of pretend
Does end as the old road
Wanders without complaint,
But emerges again,
Suddenly, without a signal,
And crashes into my eyes
With a happiness in tow.

I am the mask,
And I belong to the summer rain.

The Main Feature - "Senor Bubbles"
Also Ran - "The Then In The Now"

"The hurricane blew down the big sign from the feed store next door
And it fell across our front porch.

I ran home when Donald started to hurt the little frog.

As I hugged Maria good bye at Grand Central Station,
I didn't know it was for good.

Helen kept saying what an ugly garden it was.

I fell asleep on the couch listening to the rain sounds on the tin roof.

Bobbie Lee got mad at us because we wouldn't play with her
And said, "peepee and doodoo," right in our faces.

Oh no, they cut the big rubber tree cut down.

I forgot all my lines in the play when the house lights went out,
But they came back from nowhere when the spotlight hit me.

Dad's new Studebaker got stuck going up the hill in the red clay mud.
It was slick as ice. He blamed it on me because I wanted to see my
cousin.

Lois stole my box of crayolas, I couldn't believe it. I won't play with her
again, ever."

Yesterday is still today.
Is tomorrow packed away in this Now Box somewhere?

I'm wondering where the years are taking me
Sailing past mom and dad,
Stuck in a dream of love,
Caught in the archetypal brambles

Of childhood tumbles, scratches and tears,
Lost in the effort to believe in the "human race"
Some will make it through, some not.

Beliefs crash and burn.
I am not my body. I'm just being,
Until I can really wake up.

Getting past the karmic glue that stuck me
To this life and to some other people.
Dissolving the bindings
To free them and myself,
To spring out and fly
On the olive branch of dove's wings
Soar like the song of the eagle on
The electric blue sound of forever.

But,
Till then,
Memories return,
Rising up to the surface
And popping open like champagne bubbles,
From year One
Onward
Surprising me suddenly
With the replays of a times past.
The map of every little crook and turn in my life's path
Flickers again on memory's movie screen.
All the moments are still there,
Alive and well.
As solid as the stone wall of the cosmos.

Time Is An Errant Lover

The valentine fades slowly,
What was so hard to see,
Is still there.
It is not hidden,
But for the looking.
Still hard to see,
Up close, impossible.
The vision starts in your eyes,
And leaves through you heart's chamber door.
I miss what I thought was you,
And you miss your image of me.
Even in these aging years,
I am still eighteen.
I can't change that, my dear boy.
And if I could I would remain sixty-five
To dispel your illusions.
A sonata for the blinded hormones.

The Phantom Lover

You were just far enough off center
For your words to ensnare my imaginings.
They slipped with erotic tingles into my mouth
And bound me to the breath of life in them.

I want to ride the high wind of your thoughts.
Get lost exploring the feel of your slender tan
By sucking the boredom out of your empty moments
While I sprinkle them with cinnamon.
And slide my tongue along the memory of your body.

Sometimes your sky fills with a blue summer day,
And sometimes with a cool storm drifting.

I still walk along the empty spaces you left behind
And imagine you turning back
To reach beyond my fantasies
And fill them to float breathlessly
Above my spasms of anticipation.

Perfection is an idea that is always just ahead.
Imagining may be better than real time

Parting Regrets In The Adolescent Twinges of Old Aging

I didn't want to remember,
I didn't want to forget,
Reaching through time
The magnetic memories
Zap my present mind
With a force of urgency
And vanish.

I feel regret as the many years slip away,
But not about being wild and sexual,
Mostly about the times
I could have wrapped myself
Around some guy event
And I didn't.
My fantasy scripts become movies
That are totally blown out with such intensity
That I lay wasted and empty afterward,
Prostrate in a mindless limbo.

I realize that I am supposed to regret my
Abandonment of middle class morality,
But the average life slipped by me,
As I sidestepped it.
And came to this unusual impasse.
I gazed long, but could not see myself
In the mirror of social conventions.
And I am left with little sad feelings.
I wish I could have been a better lover,
When I was young and naïve
And still slumbered in sexual ignorance.
I didn't do all the things I wanted to,
With the some of the guys. I failed often.
The ghost of reluctance haunts me when
I think of those lost encounters.
Sorry guys, for the long list of misadventures.

Why was I so able at times
And so unable in other moments?
Not only is sex an impenetrable mystery to me,
But I am a mystery to myself.

No Lost Moments, No Lost Friends
Transformations Passing

In the deepening austerity of old age,
My heart remembers what my mind forgets.
As I look back from my leaning tower of seventy years,
I see all the people I have known well
As being mysteriously iconic,
Informative, connected, life affirming and
Encapsulated now behind wispy, veiled images of time.

Back then, I knew each one as the person standing next to me,
And now, I know them as statuesque formulations of meaning
That echo and resonate in my consciousness.

VIIIFREE FALL (Post Creative Depression)

Change Rearranging

The time of drifting,
Cutting loose from everything,
Directions not indicated,
Life on hold – suspension mode
In a paralysis grip as
Thoughts fly alone blindly.

Up and down disappears
Meridians coalesce and collapse distance.
Only time remains pushing me to reappear somehow, someway.

It is the time of floating.

Emptiness feels like darkness,
With the death of the What Was
And with the birth of the Yet Unknown

I had grown accustomed to being something again,
Comfortably resting inside a familiar somebody that was me.

Now,
Not nothing.
Not nobody again.
Where is this place?
Where am I?

The spotlight is falling on an empty stage.
Without a script on the page,
The searchlight does not yet find a home.

Chasing Symbols

Writing poetry is joyful, but unnerving.
I never quite know what's in the works.
Sometimes I'm afraid that the ink well
Has no more to give,
But there is usually something
Swimming around in the dark.
Some siren-song of words,
Some sacrosanct mischief,
That demands a good pasting to the page.
I stand so smother-close to the idea
That the light bulb sputters.
As the slippery, skittish phrases get trapped in my brain
And as thoughts soak the page, drown the war on logic,
And steal definitions carelessly from the dictionary.
I try hurriedly to write stuff down
On the back of the grocery list,
Or the telephone doodle pad
Before the pencil devours it anyway.
So, I quickly scribble the remnants that surface,
Flip open books until a idea flies up into my eye net,
And/or dredge up the pressure just behind my nervous tick.
I'll do anything classical, crude or slick
Just to make a poem talk back to me,
Give me a hard time,
Kick my butt.
Because that is not as hard
As not doing it at all.
I hate that.
It drowns my little red school house
In the swamp of a sleeping snail slime.

Word Search In Bedlam

I jump into the churning froth of consciousness
Without intent,
Get a print-out of the
Unfocused run of words
Spilling out of the toy box of my brain
Like GI Joe action dolls,
TV comic heroes that twist destiny into a pinball game
Yeah, hooray, anyway.
Delight
De way.

A cold cocked smorgasbord of mind stuffs
Itemizing itself shamelessly
Dredging up the useless and mundane
From the vacuous stream of unfocused thoughts
Scattering themselves across the blankness of the page
Recklessly hopping from one idea to another.

The frantic leapfrog search for a poem
With no start and no ending.
What's in a word?
The echo is hollow, hollow, hollow and empty.

But somehow,
The itch in the twitch of my fingers
Will spell out the next poem.

IX FISHING LINES IN THE SPIRIT STREAM

Word Wands

The words open up
And spill their life across the mind,
Printing their secrets on the photographic neurons
Of memory in winding signals,
Spiraling out of the consciousness
Into the dream theater
Lighting up the synaptic night
And raising day into being.

Lift Off

Each weighted step was a hundred years
And then I found you
Right where you've always been.
You never said goodbye.

Now, I know
I go with you through time
In my dreaming,
The day dream sails,
The night dream flies.

With The Force of Vapors

Filling all the spaces in as many faces
Your one visage contains them all
As the Everything fills a crystal ball.

You fill the many faces,
One is not enough,
Because you touch the final illusion
Weightlessly
Like falling.

Your closeness cloaks you
As though you never were
As though imagination is your only home.

You sit illusively in my thoughts that struggle to grasp you.
The heart is longing for you to be there.

You touch them all,
Drifting gently through
The dimensions,
One, Two, Three and Four,
"Ask me again
And I'll tell you more," you whisper.
"Read the sign above the ancient door."

Your touched me with my body,
You tickle these scribbles
Even as I doubt things,
You already know anyway.

And Then

As I am passing, I see
All my yesterdays and
All my tomorrows
Are woven into
The fabric of now.

As short as a second
Tumbling over itself
In perpetual motion,

I wrap the moment around myself
As the spirit's trembling blanket covers me
In the ever changing tales of time,

And reminds me that
It's time to remember
Now is forever.

Again, You Are The Mirror Is You, Again

Death is not the final divorce.
Karma laughs
As the sticky stigmata of
A new marriage reunion is tattooed
In skin tight wedding rings on the
Next incarnation of the victim and the victimizer.

And the jumping return to role reversal begins
Until the act is done again
In it's mirrored reflection.
Opposite side to opposite side
Until the rebalancing is equal
And finally, they face each other
In each others face.

That which was floating in light
Became the demon of dogma
As it drifted down through earth shear
And got penned to the page
In glitches of well meaning,
But damns the readers on the reading
In the name of goodness,
In the names of the prophets.

So, caution softly glides
Through the lives of the wise
While they taste the freshness of each new day
And find that innocence is not a lost thing,
But one that is an acquired thing,
Long sought and hard to find thing.

Tick Tock

The old days start counting themselves
Against the passing
That goes unnoticed by the clock itself.
Time does not pass,
We do.

Now You See It, Now You Don't

Shambala, Agam Des
Babaji, Rebazarr Tarz
Half in and half out of this world
Are sequestered in secret places
With granite faces.
Cities and people
Shrouded in the clouds and dreams
Shimmering behind our mortal blindness
Hanging in the air
Clinging with delicate fingers
To the higher mind.

Thoughts slanted like stairs
Climb from the seen into the ethers
Aspire on the spiral to everywhere
At the same time
Backward glance
Forward sight.
They await our homecoming
With quiet bouquets of radiance
As near as, sure is sure,
And farther back than hope lives.

The Reaping

The deafening sound of silence
Surrounds the solitary soul
With walls of frozen time
Until the death rattle
Shatters the mortal prison
And the light breaks through
The moldering halls of this last dark illusion.

Vespers

Thoughts drift quietly to the ends of space
As the incandescent evening star
Illuminates the dreaming night
With glowing highways to all possibilities.

The Crystal Whispers

Tomorrow and tomorrow
The dream fulfilled
Will spill itself
On the pages of time.

X THE PHARAOH'S MIDNIGHT JOURNEY

In ancient Egypt, a Pharaoh's initiation was effected by locking that succeeding Pharaoh in a sarcophagus for three days. This is my musings on the initiation.
Inspired by The Winged Pharaoh by Joan Grant

Prelude To Entombment

They say I am the child of the rising sun
And must walk down the hallway
Of my ancestor's blood line
Where the spirits warm the shadows
Pointing the way for me to go
As I approach my initiation
To become the pharaoh.
The Dream Quest beckons.

I will sail through sleeping eyes
To the eternal road and
Await the promptings of the lords of karma,
Even though I would rather have a good word from a friend,
A touch,
Or a kiss
Like a lost child
As I am wandering through the trembling air of my own thoughts.

The presentment of disquieting adventure
Has followed me day and night.
Time molders like an old relic.
My thirst for fulfillment
Sings a harrowing melody
As ignorance of that which is to come
Besets me and disturbs my sanctuary.

And so, I lay down
Into the bed of slumber
That is my sarcophagus.

I am drawn thru the hollow in the holes of my mind
Past the thinking, beyond the think,
I sail
To where,
To when,
I do not yet know.
I journey without will in mind's void.

Those I know fade from memory
Those I know not, arise.

I am locked in the tomb of my unconsciousness
The tomb of my dreams.
The tomb of night
Is thrust upon me.

What visions will befall me,
I cannot devine.
What shall I believe
As the spores of reality
Rain down upon the fertile lens
Of my imaginings?

What is true?
What is real?
Is it all an illusion?
Is none of it real?
Or is all of it real?

I shall see,
So, I shall see.

XI THE SURREAL LINKAGE OF THE MAGNETIC BOARD POEMS

One:

The TV Popsicle paradise chants
With a chocolate tongue apparatus
As the milky moon gown meanders through summer giggles.

Picture a puppy garden eating galoshes
As a forest friend plays mother music language
With a storm puddle poet,
And a cool blue symphony remembers to play
The dizzy slather dance.

Two:

The carnival of the sleeping weeds
Is and isn't, isn't it?
The word-motor is recalling
The as, of, to, at, by, behind, and beneath,
And is urging through, after, above, and about
To imagine that under, over, and after
Could fiddle all day in the WhoWhat River.

Three:

The anatomy of the mad diamond
Abounds with pounds of apple power,
And streams with essential singings.
Throw the urge to trudge behind voice matter
Into delirious winging winds
And elaborate on iron, rock-bed rose luck.

Four:

The lazy lizard's luscious language
Eats lunch and light alike.
The time machine is teaching
Every never moment to the carnival kid.
And the anatomy blossom recalls
Essential weeds sighing in the slippery summer.
The storm dancer stares deliriously
At the music gone wild with whispers.

Five:

The sky boy's smooth dream machine
Is thought to think that
Cool tops and cozy stops
Need orange hair to imagine
The blue glow of whispers at the circus

Six:

The solitary lounge music celebrates bare hours.
The cocktail of night lusciously smoothes over
The groaning boundaries of day,
And hums wandering breathing rhythms.
This fluff lotion train is leaving at urge time.

Six:

Rhythm bed's mad anatomy shines.
And dreams about tingle licking things,
Blossoming floods.
Whisper watch is manipulating the will drive.
Carnival of cozy paradise,
Is bound with needing plumpness.
Summer giggles piping in
Life's languid juice garden.
The sky skin motor dances.

Seven:

Petal power tells an angel
That the cheek of night
Is in the mouth garden.
It is a giggle motion moment
As the rose wind shines
On these dream plays
And a finger pole
Licks peach blossom honey.

Eight:

The sausage puddle sizzles
As mummers stagger with the luck thing
And love sky recalls elaborate purple laughter
While summer's urge imagines winter's lunch.

Nine:

TV needs chocolate with useful living
So, it searches the lazy void
Under the tingle mouth machine
And speaks to fluff dancers
That stagger when recalled.
You and I will meander through the celebrating mummers.

Ten:

Rain cheeks shine in the lizard motor
As oil drunken stones giggle
By the weed stream.
Sky feet play in the storm cocktail.
Some gorgeous iron lust
Waits to ask the thought road how to sing.

Eleven:

Incubate a lot of luscious thrill things
In some sliding candy while standing
Beside the Easy Luck Goddess who is
Throwing immense stares at
Mother Peach,
Daddy Moment,
And me, Wax Café.

XII THE ETC. MEMORANDUM

FIRST MEMO:
The Definition of Place

In case of Edgar Cayce
Think not, just relax!
Searching for the location to spill out,
And take the lid off,
Looking for the source jack to plug into,
As in, slip by the brainpower action
Walk without doors
As in sleep, but awake
To see thru the obvious
To discover the big stuff behind the picture
Breathing heavy to touch the sound
And swallow the light in one gulp
Like burn the bush
And climb the ladder
Squeeze the energy inside the matter.
Just keep writing till the walls turn to halls
And then leave.

SECOND MEMO:
A Short Fairytale For Those Who Lack A Mythology

The secret heart of the universe
Quietly waited in the janitor's closet.
The clues were in the giggles of the cherubic soap bubbles.
The sludge crept along the back stairwell
Smugly feigning an attitude of abject humiliation,
Because it seemed infinitely more applicable to this situation
And it was fun, for a change.
All things were in their heaven.
And what was not,
Flatly refused to accept E=MC2
Or quantum physics in any shape or form,
So whatever the matter didn't really matter anyway.

THIRD MEMO:
The Dos and Donts of Delightful Chaos In Focus

The pristine, crystal lens looking glass eye of the imagination
Seeing beyond concrete solidities,
That magnifying into belief
The probe of day dreaming
Sail beams thru the wall of unassailables,
Easily slipping,
Quickly streaming
On the minds holographic
Wave lengths,
Into the wonders of more worlds
Than you can shake a stick at.

Waiting patiently for the entrance of the probe
Waiting gracefully for skepticism
To mutate into a leap of faith
That is really, really there
Like you and me here
Is really, really real
Like you and me.

Although the schools of books and blunders
Say, "No,
It's only your imagination!
Toss it off.
Don't be childish
In your fantastical world of fanatical fancies."
"That's not a real world.
It's the cartoon of your vanity,
Of your silliness.
Now get back to work.
Scrub the dictionary with your toothbrush,
Retrash the recycle
And slosh the golliwogs
Because they're selling for two pounds of Dow

And six percent of the NASDAC.
No more fairytales,
No more fables,
Go get the peas back in the pod
For God's sake.
And don't listen to that woman in the moon mist.
Just because she has wings
Doesn't make her an angel."

FOURTH MEMO:
Dear Nina,

I was going to send this note by regular mail, but the wiggly stamp slipped
out from under my thumb. So, it's e-mail time. You might call this an
e-mote.

Because I need to thank you for the advice. . . You were right, in most
cases of illness homemade chocolate chips cookies may not cure the problem,
but they amply hasten the recovery.

And btw, I want to say,
Your voice divides the moment into sounds from the old scrapbook, a breath of
now, plus tomorrow's postings, gift-wrappedl in the timeless.

The divining rod in your brain waves searches out the life essence of
your friends.
Even tracking down the synaptic nerve routes in our shadows,
which we often hide inside the laundry hamper. No matter.

Your amazing discovery of a wormhole in cyberspace still has us all
wondering if it was because of extensive research, a native intuition,
or a deliberate accident.

The wind chimes of your intent fold the years into ribbons that are
intricately woven into the nests of morning doves and the like.

Your secretary, stationed as a raccoon in the woods behind your apartment,
is busy writing your schedule for the day, which you will scrupulously
observe, to folly's delight.

You habitually decline the offer from the twisted brow of sorrow
Knowing the other eventual side of its face will appear as laughter

tomorrow.
The commands of sadness fall to meaningless issue as though silenced
By your harmonious compliance to Better Housekeeping and Mad
Magazine.

The tidy tucks and easy chairs the meeting of the ceiling with the sky.
The
stairs climb to the swaying ethers and morph into delightful guesses
and
games of surprise.

Your probing reach to understand the whys in the wherefores is a good
long
stretching yawn on waking up from a deep night of dreaming.

Of course, your diary is so easy to overlook that the morning news
anchors
announce none of it, not even your giggle.

I have to stop writing now and catch the Cyberville Trolley again.
Well,
more later.

Take care, or take two aspirin (whichever one comes first.)

Mostly James

P.S. Not to mention that the goddess
Turns the dissent of tragedy to unfeeling granite,
As the lively dance of the moment
Dispels the ancient curse of sadness.
And somewhere on an Irish moor
A legend drifts across a moss-covered stone
that reads,
"Aware of nature's frail composure,
Softly through her days she sped,
While breezes sang her loving disclosure.

With insightful gaze she rallied her spells
Changing from goddess
To Fairae Queen in magical supposure.
There in the quiet shadows of the obscurity tree
She finds freedom in solitude's enclosure.

FIFTH MEMO:
What Is His Name?

I said it this morning. I knew it this morning.
And now it has slipped into the old brain shredder.
I know it's not Turhan Bey
Or flotsam bay.
Maybe the Velvet Fog
Roger Moore Rabbit
Absalom begone
Blue moon cruise
Abnay cay
Icsnay Amscray
Mel Torme. That's it.

When I was . . .
And am no more . . .
But who's keeping score.
Older than I am . . .
But not as old as I am supposed to be .

What did the Hawthorn say to the Rose?
"My galaxy is stuck to your face."

All that heaven will allow
And time will erase.
Carefully fold and
Return to the case.

SIXTH MEMO:
Quick Study of a Second Language
(for 5 to 10 year old kids only – adults not allowed)

From the galaxy of Kaoticka
On the planet of Gibber, way away,
They speak a language of exotica
Even now on this very, very day
And here on planet Earth in lots of places
We are learning this language, as fast as we can
So we will cover all of our bases.
That is the big picture, and the overall plan.
It is now spoken on Wall Street, and Capitol Hill
It is the rage in Egypt, France and Brazil
So listen and I'll speak it for you,
So you can learn to speak it too.

Abinga dinga donga flinga
Kagonga falonga manonga ablonga
Gooden laden mathen hather
Flather agrodden kladen
Smath Kothen Flodder.

Yinging minging yong wong dong
Fong long a ling ling gong
Ming nong ning

And just for a blast
Save the best for last.

Gloth Ploth Faloth Thalisk
Mokisith Klothka Losk
Shoth Floth Misthla Plotsk
Kaslocken Mothiskith balothsk.

Just read these lines aloud, and in no time at all,
Without any struggle or strife,

You'll speak perfect Gibberish
For the rest of your life.

SEVENTH MEMO:
The Unspoken

The moment froze in the void of mindlessness.
No one believed it - the day the devil died.
No one wanted to believe it.
Disbelief prevailed. The madness of the search began
Because no one really wanted to eat ice cream for eternity.

The atheists bloated in their gloating saying, "I told you so."
But the burning whispers issued from the believers
Who prophesied wondrous inanities of insanities.

And to this day no one wants to believe that the devil died last
Wednesday.
Even now the intrepid, unending search goes on.
Though backyards, microscopes and telescopes,
Thru fact and fiction novels, bios, and comic books.
Thru xrays, gamma rays and all the Rays in the phone book.
It was easier to search for the non-existent while living in denial
Than to accept existing reality,
Because, frankly, none of 'em wanted to eat ice cream forever

EIGHTH MEMO:
On The Alpha Train

I hear the rickety clack on the track
Of the ride into Nothingham by the Sea
It tells me that we are very near passing Southslumberton.
That lies on the languid shores of Loch Etherian.

The nodding slip into sleep
Crashes into a sudden snap of awakening jolts,
As spirals of thought range out spreading
Their heady nuance through choirs of unknown singers.
Who line the banks of the mounting cloud canyons
Floating past the ghost in the moonlight.
And sinuously wrap around drowsing consciousness.
The tired gray trail of numbing anesthesia
Flows through nerve meridians erasing all the messages.

It doesn't matter what I am
Or who I am,
For awhile,
At least for now.
Praise the whomever for the whatever,
And for the never, the ever, and the forever.
Yum, yum, hum, Hu and ahmen.

NINTH Memo:
Another Place Not To Go

Don't call it Work,
As soon as you do,
Me and my mule
Will sit down in the middle of the road,
Get our butts hot and dusty,
And pick out noses respectively.

Call it exquitale or tehutacan
Like it's from the Mayans or Astecs.
You know, mumbo-jumbo it around some.
Just don't use the "W" word,
Cause I'm out there
Running, racing
And I'm in the homestretch.
But what ever you do,
Don't tell me I'm working.

TENTH MEMO:
Solid Thought Thingys

There are hammers and nails,
Pencils and keyboards,
Telephones and rockets,
And so on and on stuffs.

Now,
My library shelves are crammed full,
Can't get anymore poems in there
Guess, I'll start writing on the walls.

Or, if thinking makes it so,
I'll write them in the sky
And draw invisible lines among the stars
Like astronomers do,
And make a highway through the ethers,
Filled with fantastic beings for company.
Call it Route Onandon
And it'll go
All the way through to the next county,
Beyond time and space,
Into the little town called "Big Surprises That I Know Not."

That is, if thinking makes it so.

XIIIEPISODES IN A VACUUM

The Movie Is Way Different From The Book

The silence and the quiet are married in name only.
They go their separate ways
In unequal parallels,
At different speeds
Spawning different kinds of magic.
Casting spells that make illusion
Into seeming reality.

Solid sand dunes of real world stuffs,
Comedians looking for a straight man and a punch line.

So, it seems to the captive listener
Who blindly wanders into their theaters.
Even as the ears open their doors
To hear the varying levels of cacophony,
Its tangible forces of
Bird songs, traffic flows,
Passing conversations,
And swirling wind rushes,
Dubiously flirt with the body
And trick the mind with finite games of frolic.

Sometimes the body and soul despair,
Tired of the midnight gamboling.
The thoughts of the listener rise
Like ghosts above the day
Fulfilling themselves with the howls,
Sirens, warbles, whispers and chattering
Of the ongoing sound flow.

In the midst of falling silent
The quiet yields up the dialogue
Between the outer world

And the inner dimensions.

The listener's moments
Fuse the horns and the hammers
With the cackle of the grackle
And records memories and wishes on the mind.
Their vibrancy ensnared,
Is filed away,
Photocopied and forgotten.
Body itches send signal twitches
And awaken the searching scans for more.
New musings are collected and consumed.

"Important, unimportant. Important unimportant,"
Alice asked herself, many times over,
As she walked alone in Wonderland.
No answer was forthcoming.

I say, "We need some new doomsday soothsayers,
The others were wrong.
We are still here."
Seems there is no end to silence.
Even the quiet breathlessly
Vacates the spaces in between.

Silence is the concept.
Quiet is a sometimes pacifying servant
And a sometimes demonic master.
It's all just an idea.
When the friendly servant of solitude
Becomes the demon master of loneliness,
Realities are changed.
Silence is a screaming emptiness
That drives the listener
To plunder life for something or someone to touch.

The world does not offer quiet

Or perfect silence.
Only the theory of them
It is doubtful that even death
Has a plan for either.
Action forbids them both
And only allows for the idea.

In the hush
The room surrounds me.
In the hush
Dreams are born.

On the hushness,
I travel.
I escape the earthbound bindings,
Sailing off,
Albeit doubting my own good fortune of freedom.

Destination - The Amazement Park.
And ride the vast horizon
Where potentials are inevitable
And the limitless is the food of the Gods.

Wellspring of silences in the land of the quiet
There are many wonders to come.
All things can happen.
Many roles to play,
Many stages are waiting in the wings for us

So, good listener, don you mask and costume,
I can hear the overture beginning, even now.

The Silence

Before sounds,
Before words
Was the silence ,
The embryonic rhythm of life
Incubating in the inner ear of creation.

Sometimes the silence is a friction that
Only the lonely believe,
And invisible wall of alienation
A deadly ignition of self-absorption,
An inner agreement of lostness
Pervasive in its spell
Fearing the entirety of rejection
In the pit of failing senses
Without heroes or happiness
Wedged in the absent land of the drear.

In the vaulted disappearances of silence
Flares the burning eye of light
Looking back at the distance
Preparing the sighted for its numbing clarity
Which eviscerates all contagious memories
Making them useless,
Unnecessary at last, at long last.
And plucks the dream from the dreamer
By returning it to 360 degrees of vision
Spraying miracles that flow from forever into now.

Yet, it is first thought to be a movie monster
Stunning the hopeless victims
Into insensate paralysis
And hurling them into the madness
Of dancing to the music of the spheres,
The anomaly of songs felt, but not heard,
A puppet whose strings are pulled

By the current of love's secret yearnings
Returning that which was lost to flesh
And known only to the high flying Watchers
Whose breath is the silence in the wells of contemplation.

Sanctuary in the layered veils of reality.
The winds and rains falling
Gently calling
The listener to stillness
Hypnotically smoothing, deftly soothing
The edges of the nerve ends to sleep.
The lure of emptiness
In the siren's voice of the storm.
And the distant rolling away of thunder
Numbs the random thoughts
With the ether of its rumbles.
The heart streaking flashes of lightning
Vaporize the remaining grasps for coherence.
The sizzling ear shattering explosion
Detonates the little self and
Fills the empty carcass with total surrender.

In the velvet moments, it embraces
With a lover's butterfly kisses.
Arabesques of feathered strokes
Across exhaustion in the brow.
Leaving sweet lingering phrases
Humming,
Strumming the erotic zones
And telling us that we are ignorant of our completeness
In the opiate of self-awareness.

The absolute tyranny and
The faultless demands of silence
Dissolve the composition of logic
And ignite a cataclysmic catapult
Irrational adventures,

Explorations,
Creations ,
Contact.
There is no choice here.
The bonds of the body
Burn to ashes
As the spirit is expelled
Into mindless fields of energy
Searching for anything tangible
Touchable
Seeable
Laughable
Loveable
Any light in the emptiness
Sometimes known as the wilderness.

And the quiet,
Whatever there is of it,
Is imprisoned and exsanguinated
In the depths of deep space.
He who listens to the silence
Becomes the driven.

It comes like a lover,
Like a demon
Like a game of Hide and Seek
Like a black out
Like the forgotten
Like the suddenly remembered
Like death and taxes
Like a knock on the door
Always it comes,
In whatever mask I give it,
But it surely comes.

Sometimes I wrestle with it,
Caught in its absoluteness.

Sometimes I rub it like the magic lamp
And fly away with it.

It's larger than cosmic,
Smaller than microbes.
It occupies all the air spaces,
Flows through veins and arteries,
And fills the cellular body with time.

It has an allness.
Speaking of totality.
It rules, it reigns,
This massive,
Overpowering,
Submissive
Silence that cannot be heard.
And is clearly marked
As the first road sign
On the endless highway.

The Quiet

It all began with the word, whisper.
The glassy black sheet behind me etching the voices
So very quietly on my dream
That I barely heard them.
Soft slithering sounds that sometimes
Roll into a groaning shaking
Waking within me an excitement
I cannot name.

Lay the force of hearing aside
To let the sounds enter.
Listen to the hollow
Of the empty well ringing.
To hear the silver bell sound singing.

Soon, they say, the whispers
Will clear the air
From the wells drawn down
And light the tunnel of song

Soon the flag of meaning
Will unfurl in the sureness
Of thought's reflection.
As the past moments collide
With the ever loving present.

It will not desert you.
It cannot leave.
It stays as the spine of your mythology,
The one you live by,
Drawing life to the center of its presence.
The skeletal simplicity of the moment
Holds you in its unending embrace.
It has meaning in this rapture

As you have life seeping
Into your infinity.

"Choose your words carefully" they whisper,

So, I drift lightly on the word called "breeze"
Near the edge of your shoreline
And press my fingerprints
Into the lengthening shadows of the sunset
Securing you in the tranquility of this twilight mirage.

XIV POSTSCRIPT

The days are a house of cards
That slowly collapse into yesterday.
Time grows heavier while
The avenging angle of memory descends
Into the rubble of a life lived.
Nothing is forgotten,
Nothing lost.
All is alive
In the ancient chambers of karmic ledgers.
And in the last days,
I will return to what was,
And chart what will be.

PS:
Snow White awakens from her poisoned sleep,
The chains of Prometheus fall away.
And Edgar Allan Poe smiles
As the mystic flying clipper ship
Sails through the old clock face.